the garden

All inquiries should be addressed to:
Barron's Educational Series, Inc.
250 Wireless Boulevard
Hauppauge, New York 11788

Library of Congress Catalog Card No. 91-7748

International Standard Book No. 0-8120-4708-7

Library of Congress Cataloging-in-Publication Data
Sánchez, Isidro.
    [Jardín.   English]
    The garden / I. Sánchez, C. Peris. — 1st ed.
        p.   cm. — (Discovering nature)
    Translation of: El jardín.
    Summary: Explains about plant seeds, bulbs, and flowers.
    ISBN 0-8120-4708-7
    1. Gardening—Juvenile literature.   [1. Gardening.]
    I. Peris, C. (Carme).   II. Title.   III. Series: Sánchez, I. (Isidro).
    Discovering nature.
    SB457.R4813   1991
    635.9—dc20

93-730

                91-7748
                CIP
                AC

Legal Deposit: B. 14.944-91
Printed in Spain
1234   987654321

discovering nature

the garden

I. Sánchez
C. Peris

CHILDRENS PRESS CHOICE

A Barron's title selected for educational distribution

ISBN 0-516-08453-4

It's fun helping Mom and Dad work in the garden.

We spread fresh gravel on the paths, pull up the weeds, and clean out the flower beds.

We need extra soil, seeds, flowerpots, and garden tools for our work.

Carnations and nasturtiums grow
quickly from seeds we plant in flat
boxes.

Narcissus and tulips grow from bulbs that look like onions.

Many flowers bloom in the spring. And more will grow later from the seeds that we plant now.

In the summer we move the little plants from the boxes to the flower beds. Because of the heat, the soil dries quickly, so we water very often.

In the fall we cut the plants back. This will make them grow stronger next year. We also plant bulbs that will flower in the spring.

Plants sleep during the winter. On pleasant days, we pull out the weeds and rake the ground.

The florist tells us that some houseplants don't need much light, but they should never be in a drafty place.

When we water houseplants, we must be careful not to add too much. We wash the leaves and pick off the dead ones.

We also grow new plants in flat boxes or flowerpots. In the spring and summer we will replant them in the ground or in larger flowerpots.

Now we have plants that we ourselves have grown. We can give them as gifts to our friends!

THE GARDEN

Enjoying a garden

Learning to take care of plants is a way of getting close to nature. There is the esthetic enjoyment of simply looking at flowers and foliage, as well as the satisfaction of watching what we have planted grow and thrive.

When we encourage the interest of children in plants, when we teach them the secrets of gardening, and when we help them to be sensitive to the beautiful vegetation in the world, we impart to them knowledge and appreciation of an important aspect of their culture and environment. We are helping them to be well-rounded individuals.

But, only with careful supervision will tending the home garden, the school garden, the flowerpots on the balcony or windowsill, or plants inside the home be an effective means of explaining and demonstrating the joys and rewards of gardening.

The young gardener

It would be asking too much to make children responsible for the total care of a garden. But their help can be enlisted for some important, and not very difficult, gardening tasks. They can clear the beds or plots of stones, weeds, and debris; they can plant the seeds or bulbs (with some supervision); and they can water the ground when needed, especially in warm weather when the soil is particularly dry. Thus, they will see that seeds must be planted to grow nasturtiums and that tulips grow from bulbs. They can also learn about the different stages a plant passes through during the four seasons.

Transplanting a young plant from a small flowerpot to a larger one, or to a plot or bed in the garden, involves the study of the roots and the knowledge that the plant needs soil and water to thrive. Pruning to encourage healthier foliage involves study of leaves, including an introduction to the wide variety of leaf shapes and the knowledge that the leaves capture the energy of the sun and use it to make the food the plant needs to survive. Finally, at the end of the growing season, collecting seeds involves the study of the flower's function and the knowledge that the cycle of germination, flowering, and seed gathering will resume the following spring.

Houseplants

During the winter months, interest can be focused on the many kinds of flowering and foliage plants that can be grown indoors. Poinsettias, with their spectacular scarlet bracts and strong association with the Christmas holiday season, can provide a dramatic way to capture the child's attention. A visit to the greenhouse of a botanical garden will be a revelation to children who live in cooler climates. Explain that the very same palms, ferns, and cactuses that thrive indoors in the greenhouse can be found outdoors in the warmer regions of the United States and in other subtropical and tropical areas. Follow up this outing with a visit to a neighborhood nursery where children can select their very own indoor plant to care for the year 'round.

The sense of responsibility

It is important that parents and teachers understand the role that tending a garden can play in the development of the sense of responsibility. Children should be made aware that many plants will continue to grow and thrive only if they are properly cared for; and, once the child takes on this responsibility, he or she must stay with it and not neglect this very special piece of the garden!